Local SEO

A Roadmap To Successful Local Ranking

By Tom Crandall

HangTenSEO.com

About the Author

Welcome. My Name is Tom Crandall and this is my first official SEO publication. Over the years I have authored many articles on SEO methods to help companies boost their presence on the web.

I have over 25 years experience working with and supporting the federal government, state, local agencies and local businesses with Internet and computer related projects.

Over the last 8 years I have founded 3 companies whose focus was geared towards website development, social media and SEO.

Acknowledgements

I like to personally thank my wife Kathleen Crandall for all the love and support she has given me. She has been an amazing editor and helped speed up the process of writing this book. I also would like to thank my family and friends for constant inspiration and guidance, especially my father, Chauncey Crandall III, my brothers Dr. Chauncey Crandall IV, Steve Crandall and Mike Crandall.

Lastly, I'd like to thank Olaf our pug for his commitment to being by my side during long days of writing. Actually I tend to think he was just hanging with me for food. Pugs have a tendency to be food motivated. ☺

Intro

The field of SEO is ever changing due to Google and other search engine's algorithms. What has worked in the past isn't a slam-dunk for the present or the future, so it's been my job to be as informed as I possibly can.

Local SEO has become an important aspect of a business's local footprint. Do it right and companies will see a boost in local website traffic. More often than not, I see companies completely blow it when it comes to Local SEO and as a result their potential customers find their competitors instead.

What This Book Is About

I will show you step by step how to boost a business's LOCAL website presence. I will show you the tools you will need to succeed and how to set up local business location pages for maximum exposure.

You will learn about citations, page & domain authority, paid advertising (PPC), local business listings and organic search results.

This book isn't about Global SEO, although many of the principles that I will show can help boost a website globally.

Chapters 1 -3 gives you an overview of some basic SEO concepts and provides resources to further your Local SEO knowledge.

Chapters 4 – 5 provide a little background on Local SEO and what the ranking factors are.

Chapters 6 – 15 go into the meat and potatoes of Local SEO.

Copyright © 2016 by Tom Crandall

All rights reserved. No part of this publication may be reproduced, distributed, or transmitted in any form or by any means, including photocopying, recording, or other electronic or mechanical methods, without the prior written permission of the publisher, except in the case of brief quotations embodied in critical reviews and certain other noncommercial uses permitted by copyright law.

Disclaimer

The information provided herein is stated to be truthful and consistent, in that any liability, in terms of inattention or otherwise, by any usage or abuse of any policies, processes, or directions contained within is the solitary and utter responsibility of the recipient reader. Under no circumstances will any legal responsibility or blame be held against the publisher for any reparation, damages, or monetary loss due to the information herein, either directly or indirectly.

The information herein is offered for informational purposes solely, and is universal as so. The presentation of the information is without contract or any type of guarantee assurance.

The trademarks that are used are without any consent, and the publication of the trademark is without permission or backing by the trademark owner. All trademarks and brands within this book are for clarifying purposes only and are owned by the owners themselves, not affiliated with this document.

TABLE OF CONTENTS

TABLE OF CONTENTS 8

CHAPTER 1 – SEO Terminology 9

CHAPTER 2 – SEO Software 13

CHAPTER 3 – SEO Blogs 17

CHAPTER 4 – Search Result Listings 20

CHAPTER 5 – Local SEO Ranking Factors 25

CHAPTER 6 – Domain Name Selection 27

CHAPTER 7 – Google My Business (GMB) 30

CHAPTER 8 – Keywords 35

CHAPTER 9 – Website Structure 40

CHAPTER 10 - Citation Building And Authority 49

CHAPTER 11 – Local Signals 62

CHAPTER 12 – Backlink Campaigns 64

CHAPTER 13 – Social Media And Sharing 68

CHAPTER 14 – Evaluating A Business 73

CHAPTER 15 – Local SEO Checklist 80

CHAPTER 1 – SEO Terminology

Before we dive into the basics of Local SEO, I would like to discuss some of the common acronyms, words and phrases that will be used throughout this book. My hope is after you have read Local SEO – A Road Map To Local Ranking, you will be somewhat of an expert on the subject of Local SEO and how to apply it.

- **Backlinks** – Backlinks are simply links to a website. In general the more "quality" backlinks a website receives, the higher the Domain Authority usually is.
- **Citations** – Citations are another name for a business's name, address & phone number (NAP), basically a mention of the business. An example of a citation could be a business listing in the Yellow Pages.
- **Content Marketing** – Content Marketing relates to publishing engaging content that is relevant to a particular topic or industry.
- **CTR** – Stands for Click Through Rate and is calculated based on the number of users who click on a specific link vs. the total number of users who see an ad, page or email. The

calculation is CTR = (Number of Clicks) ÷ (Number of Impressions).

- **Domain Authority** - Domain Authority is a metric (on a 100-point scale) developed by Moz (https://Moz.com) that predicts how well a website will rank on search engines.
- **Global SEO** – Global SEO represents SEO methods used to help companies and businesses target and optimize their web presence without targeting a specific geographic location.
- **GMB** – Google My Business is Google's free business listing service and is an important aspect for getting ranked locally.
- **Header Tags** – Header tags typically consist of H1 – H6 and have been determined to be part of the page rank calculation. A header tag is in the format <h1>Page Header</h1>
- **HTML** – Stands for Hypertext Markup Language and is the basic language used on most websites. Learning basic HTML is vital when performing SEO adjustments to pages. My go to source for any questions pertaining to HTML is (http://www.w3schools.com/html/)
- **Impressions** – Impressions are typically referred to as the number of times an ad

(Adwords) is viewed. Impressions are important because they help determine CTR.

- **Local Business Listing Results** – Local Business Listing Results are those listings that appear in a Google Search based on a local search query. Currently Local Business Listings appear below Paid Advertising and above Organic Searches.
- **Local SEO** – Local SEO represents SEO methods used to help companies target and optimize for specific geographic areas.
- **NAP** – Stands for Name, Address & Phone Number and is often used in conjunction with Citations. Essentially NAP is a Business's Name, Address and Phone Number for a particular location.
- **Organic Search Results** – Organic Search Results are those listings that fall underneath both paid and local business listings. A specific goal for an SEO agency is to boost a company's presence within an organic search to get to the first listing on page one. The first listing is considered to have the most relevance when searching on the web and also get the lion share of clicks.

- **Page Authority** - Page Authority is a metric (on a 100-point scale) developed by Moz that predicts how well a page will rank on search engines.
- **Paid Advertising Results** – Paid Advertising Results often referred to as PPC, are results that display at the top when a search is performed.
- **Page One** – Simply refers to the first page of the organic search results.
- **PPC** – Stands for Pay Per Click and it's an advertising method used to promote various website marketing campaigns.
- **Root Domain** - The term "Root Domain" simply means the name before the ".com or .net or …
- **SEM** – Stands for Search Engine Marketing and is typically associated with Google's PPC and other advertising efforts like Facebook, Instagram ads.
- **SEO** – Stands for Search Engine Optimization and is the basis for this book.
- **SERP** – Stands for Search Engine Results Pages that display after performing a Google, Bing, Yahoo, … search. Being at the top of page 1 is the ultimate goal of SEO for SERP listings.
- **Title Tag** – Is the HTML tag used for page titles. It is used to help determine relevance of a page's content.

CHAPTER 2 – SEO Software

SEO Gurus love their software and I am no different. To get the most out of Local SEO there are a few software tools and services I highly recommend.

- Ahrefs
- Bright Local
- Google Keyword Planner
- Moz Keyword Planner
- Moz Local
- Moz Bar
- SEO Quake
- Whitespark
- WooRank
- Yext

Ahrefs

Ahrefs (https://ahrefs.com/) is an amazing backlink, keyword monitoring service and more. Monthly plans start at $99 and go up from there. What is really cool about Ahrefs is backlink information they gather. They collect a huge index of backlink information, which you can run reports off of.

Bright Local

Bright Local (https://www.brightlocal.com) is all about Local SEO and Citation building, both of which we will discuss in much more detail in later chapters.

They have monthly plans that range from $19.99 to $64.99 (Costs may change) and a CitationBurst service that can get your company name published on some of the top Citation listing sites.

Google Keyword Planner

Google Keyword Planner (https://adwords.google.com/KeywordPlanner) is part of Google's PPC Adwords service. It's free and it helps you analyze keywords for competition, search volume, costs and other metrics. It does require you to sign up for an Adwords account (Currently it's free).

I will often use Keyword Planner in conjunction with other keyword tools such as Moz Keyword.

Moz Keyword Explorer

Moz Keyword Explorer (https://moz.com/products/pro/keyword-explorer) comes in 3 flavors: free (limited use), Level 1 ($50 per month) and Level 2 ($150 per month).

While Google Keyword Planner is free, to get the most out of Moz Keyword Explorer functionality, you will have to buy a monthly plan.

Since Moz literally wrote the book on Page and Domain Authority, they show you how competitive each word is based on these rankings. You will know almost instantly how hard it is going to be to rank.

Moz Local

Moz Local (https://moz.com/local) is Moz's Localize service where for $84 your business can get listed with the top citation listing services. Of course they don't stop there; they provide a host of other services including reporting, data exporting and distribution insights.

Moz Bar

Moz Bar (https://moz.com/products/pro/seo-toolbar) is a fantastic browser extension that provides all sorts of SEO website statistics. Moz Bar and SEOQuake are my go to extensions when performing SEO audits of pages.

SEOSiteCheckup

SEOSiteCheckup (http://seositecheckup.com/) is a website Auditing service that evaluates a websites overall SEO performance. Currently prices range from a monthly fee of $19.95 for a single site to $79.95. SEOSiteCheckup also allows one free site evaluation per day without having to pay a monthly fee. Because of this, SEOSiteCheckup is one of my go to software solutions when performing a quick site evaluation.

SEOQuake

SEOQuake (https://www.seoquake.com) is another SEO browser extension that I have come to rely on when performing any type of SEO page or website review. The data comes from SEMRush one of the top SEO businesses.

Whitespark

Whitespark (https://whitespark.ca). Whitespark has a fantastic tool called local Citation finder (https://whitespark.ca/local-citation-finder/) that searches for local citation sources. These sources help build up your local signals.

WooRank

WooRank (https://www.woorank.com/) is a website Auditing service that evaluates a website's overall SEO performance. Currently prices range from a monthly fee of $49 to $249.

Yext

Yext (http://www.yext.com/). Yext is another business citation/listing service. Currently they have established relationships with 100 business-listing providers. What makes Yext rather unique is their ability to directly integrate with these business-listing providers and push citation changes directly to them through Application Program Interface (API) calls. In many cases, changes to citations, are available real time.

CHAPTER 3 – SEO Blogs

I am always looking to improve my SEO knowledge and occasionally I find a website or blog that really stands out. The following websites and blogs are my personal favorites for SEO news and changes in the industry.

BrightLocal

BrightLocal (https://www.brightlocal.com/blog/). BrightLocal's blog is probably the best local SEO blog out there. They have a ton of fantastic articles on everything from Citation Building to Local SEO trends.

David Mihm's Blog

David has been doing SEO and involved in the Local Search industry since 2006. His blog (http://www.davidmihm.com/blog/) is a fantastic read on every Local. His also authored a rather interesting article back in 2012 that pertains to Local SEO (http://www.davidmihm.com/local-search-ranking-factors.shtml)

Hang Ten SEO

Hang Ten SEO (http://HangTenSEO.com/blog) OK a little self-promotion here. I actually write articles on SEO and I feel they are extremely informative. I use my blog as a way to really dig deep into SEO, SEM and other related topics.

Moz

Moz (https://moz.com/blog) is my go to source for all things SEO. They have a host of great writers who are knowledgeable on a vast number of SEO related subjects.

Search Engine Land

Search Engine Land (http://searchengineland.com/) is one of the leading daily publications on search marketing and SEO industry. Editor-In-Chief Matt McGee an SEO guru in his own right oversees the editorial staff. They usually have at least 3 articles a day and sometimes more.

SEMRush

SEMRush (https://www.semrush.com/blog/). These guys know SEO and have a fantastic lineup of great article writers.

Whitespark

Whitespark (https://whitespark.ca/blog/). I don't have as much experience reading their blog, but like BrightLocal, Whitespark is all about Local SEO and appears to have many articles talking about their product and what it can do to help boost your local SEO.

Yoast

Yoast (https://yoast.com/seo-blog/) If you have a Wordpress website, you will want the Yoast Plugin by

Joost de Valk. Joost's blog covers a wide range of SEO topics, but their bread and butter is Wordpress.

CHAPTER 4 – Search Result Listings

Whenever you perform a Google Search, Google's algorithm takes over and provides result listings that best match the criteria according to Google's page and domain ranking factors.

The results are broken out by:

- **Paid Advertising (PPC)** – Shown at the top and bottom of the listings with a little [Ad] next to the link. These are referred to as PPC (Paid Per Click ads) and each time they are clicked the owner of the ad gets charged. This is one of the many ways Google makes money and the reason why they have become such a dominant force in the Search Industry.
- **Local Business Listing Results** – Local Business Listing Results from Google Maps
- **Organic Search Results** – All other results that are not paid advertising or local search results.

Paid Adverting (PPC)

While paid advertising is certainly a method many business use for marketing purposes, it often can be quite expensive and the return on investment isn't always assured.

Local Business Listing Results

Local Business Listings are currently shown in what is referred to as the local three-pack, essentially 3 local listings with the option to view more places. The listings include a map, directions and a website link. It has been shown that companies listed locally generally outrank both paid and organic searches for CLRs.

Google has also implemented paid advertising for companies who want to jump ahead of the pack in local listings. It works in a similar fashion to how the current Adwords advertising works, except these new adds display when the "more places" is clicked from the three-pack listings.

Organic Search Results

Placing high in the Organic search listings requires constant monitoring and consistently new content. Many companies simply do not have the time or resources to battle their competitors in the organic search arena.

That's where I come in, to help boosts companies using various SEO techniques and methods that have been shown to increase traffic and CTR. The SEO services, depending on what companies want, can range from a few hundred a month to thousands of dollars. Most of the SEO services require a monthly plan and in general need 3-6 months of SEO campaigns before significant improvements can be made.

Local SEO

Local SEO is relatively straightforward and is usually much less than paid or organic search approaches. Local Search results also tend to have what I consider a Trust Worthy factor that Paid and Organic search results lack. People who want to buy or support local, will often go straight to the Local Business Listings before clicking on the Paid or Organic Searches.

Global SEO

Global SEO is the general concept to help improve a website's presence on the web without specifying a specific geographic location. Both Local SEO and Global SEO go hand in hand when trying to promote a page or website to the world.

With Global SEO, the goal is usually to boost the organic results of an article or website, rather than boosting its local presence.

Changing Trends In Local Searches

Initially Local Searches displayed in what was referred to as a 7 pack. This basically means there were up to 7 local listings displayed. Next came the 3 pack, where Google reduced the number to 3 top listings. Google has changed the their algorithm again, to include 1 PAID advertisement. This is now called the 2 Pack, 2 local listings + 1 PPC listing.

Mobile

Mobile has become the dominant search method and Google is now rewarding websites that are mobile friendly. The other advantage to mobile is the ability to determine exact location and use this information for more accurate local searches.

What This Book Will Cover

In this book, we are only going to focus on Local SEO Listings within a Google search and how to improve a business's chance of showing up in the top 2 spots. A side benefit of performing Local SEO is that it can improve a website's Domain Authority and in turn boost both page and website organic search rankings.

We are not going to delve into Paid Per Click (PPC), but that is certainly another method to help boost your visibility in searches.

CHAPTER 5 – Local SEO Ranking Factors

There are 8 main factors that help websites rank locally when searched.

These include:

- Domain Name Selection
- Google My Business (GMB)
- Website Structure
- Keywords
- Citation Building and Authority
- Local Signals
- Backlink Campaign
- Syndication and Sharing

While the above are my own Local SEO Ranking factors that I have determined to be extremely beneficial to ranking LOCALLY, you may want to also check out the following.

- **Moz – The 2015 Local Search Ranking Factors** (https://moz.com/local-search-ranking-factors)
- **Search Engine Land – How To Rank Your Local Business** (http://searchengineland.com/local-seo-rank-local-business-218906)

Also note that what currently works now may not work in the future. Google and other search engines have a tendency to change their algorithms that can and will effect how pages rank.

In the next 10 chapters we are going to explore how each of these factors help overall local ranking.

CHAPTER 6 – Domain Name Selection

For those who haven't decided on a Domain name and only have one office, selecting a Keyword Rich Domain Name that is geared towards local searching, can help increase your chances of being listed as a local business.

For example if I have a business that I want to rank for and it's located in Austin, Texas, I would want to create a root domain that includes the city "Austin" as part of the URL. The term "Root Domain" simply means the name before the ".com or .net or ..."

Let's take this a step further. Beyond location name, you also want to include at least one of your KEYWORDS in your URL. If I have a Chiropractic office located in Austin, I might choose the domain "AustinChiropractic.com". Unless you are really fortunate, the domain that makes sense for your business might be taken, so you will have to be a bit more creative when coming up with a domain name.

Domain Name Search

If you visit Godaddy (https://www.godaddy.com/), the home page gives you the ability to perform a domain name search. When the results are returned it will tell you whether the domain is available or already taken.

Further more Godaddy will give you alternative domain names to choose from.

Domain Name Selection

Ultimately a domain name selection really boils down to your business model. Google, Amazon, Twitter and others obviously don't have a keyword or location in their domain name, but will probably still do well in localized searches if they are pursuing that for their various offices.

Also some businesses have multiple locations, so this technique isn't optimal in those situations. If your business is in multiple countries, you will want to have a neutral or generic domain structure that doesn't contain location information.

Multi Location Businesses AND Established Branded Domain Names

For businesses that have multiple locations or for businesses that already have an established name or a branded domain name, another technique is used. Instead of worrying about the Domain name, specific pages are created to target the geographic areas the offices are located in.

For example Whole Foods has locations all around the US, so to compete on a local level, Whole Foods has created specific pages for each store location. Here in

Austin, one of the Whole foods locations is called the Domain and its URL is "http://www.wholefoodsmarket.com/stores/domain". As you can see, the location is part of the URL.

My preference with respect to Whole Foods would have been to include Austin after Domain. It would look something like this "http://www.wholefoodsmarket.com/stores/domain-austin". By including Austin in the URL it may boost the chances for the page to rank higher for the keyword "Austin".

Whole Foods has taken the concept of local SEO even further by creating micro locations within some of their stores. The Whole Foods Headquarters actually has several unique restaurants within the store. Each of these restaurants now has it's own Google My Business listing. As a result of segmenting out the individual restaurants from the main store, they have boosted their website traffic and their local SEO rankings.

CHAPTER 7 – Google My Business (GMB)

Google My Business (https://www.google.com/business/) is Google's answer to local listings and has become the de facto way for a business to be listed locally. Not being listed on Google My Business will almost certainly mean you will not show up for localized searches, at least via a Google search.

When you setup an account with Google My Business you're letting Google and customers know you are open for business. It helps you instantly stand out, whether people are looking for you on Google's Search or Maps.

When creating the account Google will ask for various fields to be filled out, but the most important fields include

- Business Name
- Address
- City
- State
- Country
- Postal Code
- Primary Phone
- Website Categories

Consistency | NAP | Citation

The information above is often referred to as NAP or a Citation and is used both on-page for On-page signals and off-page for NAP consistency.

It's important when setting up a Local SEO campaign to have the NAP be consistent across a business's citation listings. In other words you want to use the same Business Name, Address and Phone Number information for each citation.

Important: Keep track of the Business Name, address and phone number because you will need that information when setting up your website for local SEO.

Categories

When you initially setup a Google My Business account, Google will prompt you to choose a category. The category represents a description of what your company is.

Back in 2013 Google changed how categories are created. Essentially Google eliminated the option of using custom categories.

For my company, Hang Ten SEO, Google doesn't give the option to choose "SEO" or "Search Engine Optimization". Your options are limited to Google's fixed list of choices.

I ended up choosing "Internet Marketing Consultant". Prior to 2013, I could have chosen something more Local SEO friendly like "Internet Marketing Consultant in Austin", which I have seen other companies use.

Depending on your company and your brand, you may have to do what I did and choose the closest definition of what you do. After you have created your initial category and business listing, you will have the option to add other categories to your business.

In my case I also added the category "Website Designer", which makes sense because I will often create Wordpress Websites for clients.

Important: Keep track of the Google My Business (GMB) Category names you have selected because you will need those names when setting up location pages and URL structures.

For example I might want to create a page called "http://HangTenSEO/Internet-Marketing-Consultant-Austin-Tx" and another one http://HangTenSEO/Website-designer-Austin-Tx.

As you can see the URL contains both the Category and Location, which has been shown to help boost local ranking scores over business that haven't included this information.

Get Verified

Once you have setup a Google My Business account and entered the required information, you will have to prove that your company actually has a physical location. To do this, you have to request verification post card from Google (normally it takes between 1 to 2 weeks to receive it). Once received, you can log into your Google My Business account and enter the verification code, which verifies your business address.

Address Listing

After your Google My Business account is all setup and verified, when someone searches for your company on Google, your business will show up in at least 2 locations. First you should see your company's website in the organic search listing on the left.

Second a new information box about your company will display on the right, allowing people to read and post reviews.

This second box actually makes your company look very professional and legit. A win/win for your efforts.

CHAPTER 8 – Keywords

In SEO terms, keywords represent words or phrases people use to perform searches that make it possible to find your website. Optimizing your website for specific keywords and phrases increases the likelihood that someone who uses those keywords or phrases will ultimately find your page or website over someone else's.

Before writing an article, putting up a website or choosing a domain name, you should start thinking about how people are going to discover the article, the website or business.

What words or phrases are they going to use when searching? This concept is known as Keyword Research and it is a way to help establish a baseline from which to build content.

Keyword Analysis Tools

There are a host of keyword analysis tools to help perform keyword research. Here are a few I use:

- Google Auto Complete (Auto complete results from the Google search bar)
- Google Adwords Keyword Planner (https://adwords.google.com/KeywordPlanner)
- Google Trends (https://www.google.com/trends)

- Moz Keyword Explorer (https://moz.com/explorer)
- Uber Suggest (https://ubersuggest.io/)

What you are looking to determine is how competitive a particular keyword or phrase is and what the search volume is. If a keyword is really competitive, that will tell you that it will be hard to rank for, in other words it will be hard to compete against other articles and websites for that specific keyword. Search volume represents how many people are actually searching on the keyword or phrase in a given month. The more people who are searching, the more traffic that keyword or phrase potentially brings with it.

The ideal keyword or phrase is one that has low competition and high monthly searches. Unfortunately for a lot of businesses in competitive industries, going after these unicorns is quite a challenge.

Long Tail Keywords

A "Long Tail Keyword" is a set of keywords grouped together to form a phrase. The advantage of Long Tail Keywords is they aren't as competitive as a single keyword is.

For instance I wrote an article where one of my target long tail keywords was Best Balance Boards. My thinking was that I probably wouldn't be able to rank for the more competitive term "Balance Boards", but I might be able to rank for "Best Balance Boards". Adding the term Best obviously made a difference. Now if you search for Best Balance Boards or Best Balance Board, my article usually shows up on page one of Google. You can also search for "Top Balance Board" and the article is usually in the top 5 of Google.

The biggest advantage of using a Long Tailed Keyword approach is there isn't as much competition, thus each phrase is easier to rank for. Another advantage is you can actually target multiple Long Tail Keywords in the same article. Many SEO professionals use the Long Tail Keyword approach to help boost an article's ranking and eventually rank for the shorter head terms words. The reason for this is rather straight forward, as a website gains traffic and backlinks through the Long Tail Keywords, the Page Authority or Page Ranking improves, which in turn improves ranking for the more competitive keyword.

Another advantage to Long Tailed Keywords is they are usually highly specific and tend to draw more quality hits to an article or page, which leads in more conversions.

Local Keywords

With Local Keywords you're taking the concept of Keyword Analysis and Long Tail Keywords and applying it locally.

There are thousands of SEO companies around the world, but there probably are only a handful in a particular city. As an SEO company, I can then start applying local keywords to my SEO business to form Long Tail Keywords. These then are even less competitive than my balance board example because the phrase is filtered down a specific location.

I could take the phrase "SEO Services", which is a highly competitive phrase and add "Austin", to make "Austin SEO Services" or simply "Austin SEO".

Focused Keyword

Whenever you write an article or add a page to a website, the content should always be focused around a main keyword or phrase. This is often called the Focused Keyword and it is the keyword you ultimately want to rank for.

In Wordpress, there is a plugin called "Yoast SEO for WordPress" that uses the focused keyword and gives an overall page score based on usage and various ranking factors like header tags, title tags, content, length of content and so on.

View The Top 10

When I have finalized my keyword list, I normally like to see what actually shows up when I perform a Google Search. I will go through a few questions to get a feel for how well I think my selection will do. I ask questions such as:

- Do I feel I can rank from the results that are listed?
- How long are their articles or pages?
- What are the Domain and Page ranking scores?

If based on my analysis, I feel I can't rank, then I will start the process all over again and look for another permutation.

Bottom Line

Choosing the ultimate keyword isn't an exact science and sometimes the keyword choice fails to produce results. Even when your content and your keywords are in total harmony, you may still have a hard time ranking if your website is new or you have a low domain authority.

CHAPTER 9 – Website Structure

To recap, in Chapter 6 we talked about how it's advantageous to weave the City or County you service into your domain name. If that isn't practical because you already have a domain name or have multiple business locations, you still want to have the city or country be part of the URL structure. Taking Hang Ten SEO's website as an example, if I wanted to service Austin locally, which I do, I would create a page called

Example 1: http://HangTenSEO.com/SEO-Austin/

or

Example 2: http://HangTenSEO.com/Locations/SEO-Austin/

as opposed to

http://HangTenSEO.com/SEO/

Notice I have the city on both examples. Example 2 is a better setup for businesses that have multiple locations and in general is a good URL structure.

Local Business Landing Page

After deciding on the proper URL structure, it's time to get busy creating a Local Business Landing Page.

When building your local business landing page or pages (1 for each location), you want to include 12 basic areas to help boost your Local business rankings. These areas are broken into 2 main sections including the Local Business Page and the Sidebar. For websites that don't have sidebars, you may be able to put the sidebar information on the page or maybe in the footer. Many WordPress templates (My Preference Is WordPress), allow you to create multiple sidebars depending on the page you are on.

The information that you create may not look as nice or as pretty as you want it to be, but remember, this page is more for ranking your Business in local searches rather than winning awards for looks. Companies that don't take this approach will most likely not rank as high and will have a harder time getting into the 3 pack local listings.

(1) About Your Business

In this section you want to include localized words such as the city and state where your business resides. You will also want to include the Google My Business categories, plus any other categories that might relate to your business, but aren't part of the Google My Business category listings.

(2) Video

Google and most search engines seem to like having videos as part of the content and tend to rank them higher. It's a good idea to make sure the video is from Youtube, since it's a Google owned company, which may give the page a bit higher ranking vs. another video source. Each Video should include the business name, category, city and state for the Title, Tags and Description. All this information can be added via Youtube's interface.

(3) Images

Each local business page should contain at least one image. The image's name should contain the business name, category, city and state where the business is located. Google and other search engines seem to favor pages that have multimedia over ones that don't.

(4) Services We Provide

In the Services We Provide section you are just looking to include your Google My Business Categories and the City and State where the business is located.

(5) Our "Business" Services

In the Our "Business" Services section you are looking to include all the services that your company performs at the highest level without getting too detailed. In my case, I used "Our SEO Services", since SEO is what I do and then listed the various services.

(6) Proudly Serving

The proudly serving section is all about adding local signals. In this area it's a great idea to link up to a city's .gov website. Taking this a step further you can also link up to other surrounding cities you may service. For example since I live in Austin, I choose to link to Austin, Lakeway, Round Rock, Georgetown and Bastrop.

Local signals help Search Engines establish that you are tied into the local community vs. being a national or global brand.

Side Bar

For Contact, Directions, Office Hours, Near By Places, and Reviews, I will often place these items on the sidebar. It's more of an aesthetic approach, but it seems to work quite well.

(7) Contact

In the contact section you're listing your Google My Business address information for your business. This section should use schema.org data HCard Format. (http://microformats.org/wiki/hcard)

Hang Ten SEO

1825A West 11th Street

Austin, TX 78703

512.413.8143

info@HangTenSEO.com

In my case the code for the HCard address information looks like this:

<div class="vcard">

<div class="org">Hang Ten SEO</div>

<div class="adr"><div class="street-address">1825A West 11th Street</div>

<span class="locality">Austin</span>,

<span class="region">TX</span>

<span class="postal-code">78703</span></div>

<div class="tel">512.413.8143</div>

<a class="email" href="mailto:info@HangTenSEO.com">info@HangTenSEO.com</a>

</div>

(8) Directions

For the directions section my preference is to use the Google Maps iframe code for my business location. It looks something like this:

<iframe src="https://www.google.com/maps/embed?pb=!1m1

8!1m12!1m3!1d2411.0645157688155!2d-97.76563805340284!3d30.28276912413652!2m3!1f0!2f0!3f0!3m2!1i1024!2i768!4f13.1!3m3!1m2!1s0x8644b54243a384ef%3A0x13695a717349eaad!2s1825+W+11th+St%2C+Austin%2C+TX+78703!5e0!3m2!1sen!2sus!4v1472586316259" width="300" height="150" frameborder="0" style="border:0" allowfullscreen></iframe>

Don't worry the code above is auto generated by Google.

- Simply go to Google Maps, enter your address information.
- When the little red pin marker appears on the map, click the "Share" Button.
- A modal window will appear displaying the map, click the Embed Map tab and copy the iframe code and paste it into your sidebar.
- You can adjust the size of the map by changing the width and height parameters within the iframe code.

(9) Office Hours

Including office hours is another signal that Google can look at. It's there to boost your business listing presence. Having office hours also gives the impression that you are a real business.

(10) Near By Places

Near by places are additional local signals that you're telling Google to look at. Again the goal is to show Google that your business is local. You should pick restaurants and hotels that are near your business location.

(11) Reviews

While I didn't include reviews in the image above, reviews are now part of Google's equation to boost your local business's overall ranking score. A great place to include reviews is on the sidebar above office hours. Reviews should be in the form of Review HCard Format.

You will want to make sure people can review your company on Google Reviews and Yelp (https://biz.yelp.com/), both of which will require that you establish a Google My Business Page and a Yelp For Business Owners Page.

(12) Google My Business Categories

When creating a Google My Business account, you have to specify at least 1 category. Each of these categories should have their own page, similar to the Local Business Landing Page above. These categories should be listed on the sidebar as links to their respective pages. This will help boost the Business Page's Authority.

The technique that is being applied is sometimes called Siloing or building a Silo of internal links for each category. Your Local Business Landing Page will usually have at least one, but maybe 2 or 3 additional pages that pertain to each category. In some cases you can even have links that go deeper into your web structure. Think of it as your own Wikipedia.

(13) Titles, Meta Description and Header Tags

Be sure that you include both the city and keyword in your title tag, Meta Description and at least 1 header tag. While the Meta Description will not help you rank, it does help in CTR (Click Through Rate) when people are looking for local businesses.

CHAPTER 10 - Citation Building And Authority

Citation Building and Authority revolve around the mentions of your business name, address and phone number, also known as NAP. It can include both backlinks to your website and plain text.

Consistency Is The Key

Important: One of the most important aspects of NAP is consistency. Having different variations of a business's name, address and phone number will negatively effect the citation's authority score and hurt a company's overall ranking. Using "street" instead of "st" or omitting suite or unit numbers can cause issues. Search engines may not know which is the correct version and might use the version that doesn't have a lot of authority.

Conduct A Citation Evaluation

Whenever I take on a client for citation building efforts, the first thing I do is get a baseline of their existing citations. I look at 4 main areas including:

- Known Citation Listings
- Incomplete Citations Listings
- Inconsistent Listings
- Duplicate Listings

This becomes my baseline from which to work with. In many cases the baseline can be rather small, especially if the business is just starting out or hasn't performed a lot of Local SEO efforts.

It's something the client can sink their teeth into and it's where I can show progress once I start working with them.

I find that Moz Local's citation search tool (https://moz.com/local/search) is perfect for performing these citation audits.

Keep A Record

When starting a citation building campaign it's a great idea to have an excel spreadsheet or some other method to track the Business Name, Address and Phone Number. Remember it's very important that you only use one variation for each location. Having inconsistent listings across the web will hurt your ability to rank.

You will also want to keep track of any user names and passwords you may have to create when managing your NAP on business listing sites. Below are just a few websites that are good to start with.

- Acxiom
- Citysearch
- Facebook
- Factual
- Foursquare
- Google My Business
- Hotfrog
- Localeze
- Superpages

- YP
- Yelp

In order to setup most local Business Listing Pages (Citations) you will want to have the following information available.

- Name Of Business
- Address
- Phone Number
- Email
- Website Address
- Social Media Accounts for (Twitter, Facebook and LinkedIn)
- A paragraph or 2 that describes the business
- Primary Category (Used From Google My Business)
- 4 to 5 pictures
- Business Filing Information
- Verification Email and Phone Number

Note: Again it's important to be consistent when creating new citations.

Manually Building Your Citations

When first starting a citation building campaign, manually creating your citations may sound like easy way to get your name out there, but it can quickly become very time consuming and often very frustrating effort.

Each Business Listing site has their own quirks and policies on how a listing is created. There isn't a one size fits all method to really streamline the process.

Most sites require some form of validation and usually require a local phone number, the local address to send a validation card to and sometimes actual proof of business documents.

For example Acxiom (http://www.acxiom.com/) requires one of the following.

- Federal Tax License Letter (submit the letter that includes your id number, name, address and/or phone number of business)
- State, County, or City Business License or Sales Tax License
- Doing Business As License
- Fictitious Name Registration

Another problem you will run into is actually trying to contact many of the listing companies to help you with questions you may have. I have submitted numerous support tickets that simply go unanswered and you can forget about reaching a live person via phone.

Citation Building On Auto Pilot

If you dread the thought of manually creating numerous accounts for your business. Moz Local and BrightLocal offer paid services that can do the work for you.

Currently Moz charges $87 per business location and BrightLocal charges $3 per listing, giving a discount for bulk purchases.

Both Moz and BrightLocal seem to give good service and can get your business up and running with multiple citation listings for under $100.

Structured Citations

Citations are broken down into Structured and Unstructured.

- **Structured Citation** - A structured citation would be a listing on professional listing services such as Google My Business, Yelp or the Yellow Pages (YP) (essentially directories and business listing websites).
- **Unstructured Citation** - An unstructured citation might be a mention on someone's website with your business name and possibly your phone number and address, but no real listing structure.

Citation Authority

Citation Authority involves the ranking of each citation, similar to page rank or domain rank. A citation that has a higher rank/authority relative to other citations will carry more weight when determining an overall Local ranking score.

The goal of local SEO when it comes to Citation Building and Authority is to outrank your competitors, not by having more citations, but by having higher-ranking quality citations.

Know Your Competition

When starting a citation building campaign you need a way to gauge not only your own citations, but also your competitors.

Right now 2 companies stand out in Citation Building efforts and include BrightLocal (https://www.brightlocal.com/) and Moz (https://moz.com/local/search). Both are really good companies and have various reports to help you get a handle on your citation building efforts.

I really like BrightLocal right now with the competition information they provide. If you are working with a single location, their monthly $19.95 plan is perfect. If you have multiple locations, then a more costly plan will be needed.

Moz Local's – Check My Listing (Citation Audit) search is excellent and gives you an overall score on your citation building efforts. The fact that the citation audit aspect is free makes Moz Local a no-brainer.

Currently the free Moz Local "Check My Listing" search and gives you some great overall feedback on your business listings to include:

- Completed Listings (Primary Sources, Direct Networks and Indirect Networks)
- Incomplete Listings
- Inconsistent Listings
- Duplicate Listings

A way you can use the Moz service (https://moz.com/local/search) to check on a business's competition is to simply search on the competition name rather than your own business name.

BrightLocal currently offers a free 14-day trial, so you can kick the wheels a bit. One of their reporting tools is called Google Local Wizard and it allows you to view your competitor's Citation rankings for specific keywords.

The Google Local Wizard report displays:

- Business Name
- Number of Citations
- Citation Authority
- Number of Links
- Website Authority
- Reviews
- Images
- Categories

Summary   Austin SEO   SEO Austin

Top 10 result for "SEO Austin"   (search location: 78703)

Rank	Company Name	Citations	Citations Authority	Links	Website Authority	Reviews & (Rating)	📷	Categories
A	Austin SEO Company ✓ Verified	123	58/100	163	26/100	0 (0/5)	3	Marketing Agency
B	Complete Web Resources ✓ Verified	175	57/100	318	38/100	19 (5/5)	15	Downtown
C	NuArtisan ✓ Verified	112	64/100	109	21/100	5 (4.8/5)	7	Internet Marketing Service
D	TastyPlacement ✓ Verified	256	53/100	5,167	50/100	15 (4.7/5)	50	Internet marketing service in Austin
E	Geek Powered Studios ✓ Verified	144	60/100	1,761	42/100	4 (5/5)	8	Internet marketing service
F	Moxie SEO Austin ✓ Verified	134	55/100	75	25/100	2 (5/5)	29	Internet Marketing Service
G	LifeBlood SEO Austin ✓ Verified	0	N/A	1	7/100	0 (0/5)	16	Internet Marketing Service
H	SEO Services Austin ✓ Verified	97	54/100	3	13/100	0 (0/5)	2	Internet Marketing Service
I	Austin SEO Geeks ✓ Verified	161	63/100	4	14/100	10 (5/5)	3	Marketing Consultant
J	ArtsWorks SEO ✗ Unverified	39	61/100	449	35/100	0 (0/5)	1	Internet Marketing Service

In the report above I ran a Google Search for "SEO Austin", which showed the top companies with their citation information. This gives you an idea of what needs to be done in order to possible rank above the companies listed.

One neat feature of the report is it shows the competition's Google My Business Categories, giving you insight into how each company positioned themselves for citations.

This one report is a gold mine of intel. Obviously Austin SEO Company who does have Austin in their domain name appears to dominate the listing by having lots of citations, high website authority and numerous backlinks and reviews.

A company trying to outrank Austin SEO Company would really have to work hard to beat them. If I were advising a company, I would want them to start a review and backlink campaign to boost both their website authority and review (rating) score.

Domain	Authority	Count	You	A	B	C	D	E	F	G	H	I	J
Number of citations:			3	123	175	112	256	144	134	0	97	161	39
sv-se.facebook.com	100	2				Y	Y						
local.yahoo.com	100	8		Y	Y	Y	Y	Y	Y		Y		Y
youtube.com	100	3							Y		Y	Y	
linkedin.com	100	6			Y	Y	Y	Y	Y			Y	
pinterest.com	100	5		Y		Y	Y	Y			Y		
facebook.com	100	7			Y	Y	Y	Y	Y			Y	Y
docs.google.com	100	2							Y		Y		
google.com	100	1					Y						
plus.google.com	100	6		Y	Y			Y			Y	Y	Y
chocolatejacuzzi.tumblr.com	99	1									Y		
m.youtube.com	99	1									Y		
austin-seo.tumblr.com	99	1									Y		
bloomberg.com	99	2				Y		Y					

When running the BrightLocal Google Local Wizard, a second report I have found really useful, breaks out each citation and shows you where it is listed and how many of the competitors from the first report are using it. The report has clickable links, allowing you to open up the competition's specific citation pages and see what they did.

As you can see, citation building can be quite a task. Rather than manually going to all these sites to get your business listed, you can use services like Moz Local or BrightLocal to push out your citation information.

Moz Local's pricing structure is $84 per location. If you have a business with a single location or just a few, Moz might be a great option for creating citations for your business.

BrightLocal uses what they call "Citationburst" to build citations around a business location. Each listing If you don't use services like Moz or BrightLocal, you will have to add this information in manually, which can take a very long time. A quick way to at least get your name out there is to setup a Google My Business account and also a Bing Places account.

Citation Authority

As stated previously, Citation Authority involves the ranking of each citation, similar to page rank or domain rank. A citation that has a higher rank relative to other citations will carry more weight when determining an overall Local ranking.

2 great tools for determining Citation Authority are Moz Bar and SEOquake, which I have written a lengthy article on (http://hangtenseo.com/mozbar-seoquake-seo-browser-extensions/).

The browser tools tell you what the page rank and domain rank are for the webpage you're viewing. You can use these tools when looking at Citations, to see what their overall Authority might be.

When using the Mozbar the two key elements that display when a page first loads are PA (Page Authority) and DA (Domain Authority). These values provide a really quick estimate of what the page's overall ranking might be. The higher the PA and DA are, the higher the page will typically rank when searched. This applies to both local and world wide searches.

When viewing a Citation page (A mention of your business), the PA and DA will give you a quick idea of that citation's overall ranking or Citation Authority.

For the companies who create or have citations created for them, they often overlook a very valuable aspect to citations. They simply stop at creating the citation and move on to the next citation and so forth. The key element that is missing, is…wait for it…**Page Authority**.

In most cases, when a citation is created, even on a high Domain Authority website like Yahoo or Yelp, the Page Authority for that citation is extremely low.

Boosting Citation Authority

The goal of boosting your citations is to increase the page rank, which in turn should increase its authority when pointing to your business. This method is referred to as backlinking, but instead of backlinking to your website or a page on your website, you're backlinking to your citation.

What if I have 100 Citations, will I have to do this for all of them?

It's usually a good idea to perform a backlinking campaign for the top 10 to 15 citations that have a high Domain Authority. Beyond that you're probably looking at diminishing returns on time spent doing this.

Below is an example of how Austin SEO Geeks is using the backlink strategy to boost their Yelp Citation within one of their Youtube video descriptions.

In reviewing Austin SEO Geeks, their YouTube channel contains many YouTube videos with the term Austin, their phone number and SEO as parts of the title.

When adding a video to your local business page, having a video title containing localized words can influence a local business's page ranking score.

The question remains whether search engines will ever penalize companies who create backlink campaign to their citations. My guess is probably not, since many of the websites that are linking to them are high domain authority sites.

CHAPTER 11 – Local Signals

Geo Targeted Citations

Google is becoming increasing granular when it comes to local SEO. One of the biggest driving factors is mobile searching. With mobile dominating the search sphere, Google and others are now starting to utilize the GEO capabilities down to the city block and surrounding neighborhoods.

When you are on your mobile device you can search for stores and services near your location simply by typing:

- Closest
- Near Me
- Nearby
- Open

So for example I could type Gas Stations Near Me and a list of gas stations will display that are close to my GEO location. This assumes of course that I have my GPS turned on.

Local Signals is all about building your brand locally by creating citations and backlinks in your community.

A great service for local citation building is WhiteSpark (https://whitespark.ca). One of the key tools they have searches for local citation sites. Again the concept here is showing Google and others your business is actually a local establishment with local presence.

The way Whitespark's citation tool (https://whitespark.ca/local-citation-finder/) works is you enter in your business's:

- Country
- Location
- Key Phrase

Once entered, the tool then returns potential local citation sources. It also shows the top ranking businesses with their rankings and number of citations. There are numerous links in which you can dig further into the data to learn much more about both your own and your competition's citations.

CHAPTER 12 – Backlink Campaigns

Ever wonder how the SEO Pros always seem to achieve high ranking high domain authority websites.

The key to their success almost always revolves around a GREAT backlinking strategy.

Developing Backlinks is often referred to as Inbound Marketing. There are two types of backlinks

- Follow
- nofollow

What is a Follow Link?

A follow link is a link that passes link juice to the page or website it is pointing to. Normally follow links improve PageRank and Domain Rank scores.

What does a "FOLLOW" link look like?

In HTML, a follow link looks something like this

<a href="http://www.yourwebsite.com/">Link Text</a>

Notice it's doesn't contain the rel="nofollow" element.

What is a No Follow Link?

A no follow link is a link that doesn't provide what is referred to as link juice, it doesn't boost PageRank and it doesn't improve a sites ability to move up in SERPs.

What does a "nofollow" link look like?

In HTML a nofollow link looks something like this
<ahref="http://www.yourwebsite.com/" rel="nofollow">Link Text</a>

The nofollow element tells Search Engines don't count this link as a ranking factor.

Are nofollow backlinks Worthless?

Certainly not, even though they don't provide ranking bonuses, no follow backlinks can still can bring in lots of referral traffic to your website.

Overall the best backlinks from a ranking standpoint are from high Page Authority & High Domain Authority sites that are "Follow".

When building out your local presence, you are going to want to perform 3 types of backlink campaigns.

- Non Geo Traditional Backlink Campaign
- Localized Backlink Campaign
- Citation Backlink Campaign

Before you start on any backlink campaign, I would suggest using one of the backlink tools to get a starting base line.

- Ahrefs (https://ahrefs.com/)
- Cognitive SEO Explorer (http://explorer.cognitiveseo.com/)
- SEM Rush (https://www.semrush.com)
- Moz –> Open Site Explorer (https://Moz.com)

Non Geo Traditional Backlink Campaign

A traditional backlink campaign is time intensive and often requires a lot of interaction with companies who will essentially promote your business's website or brand by providing a link on their website. There are various methods you can use during a backlink campaign including:

- View Your Competitor's Backlinks and Reach Out To The Websites That Point Back To The Competitor.
- Publish Long Content (Passive Link Building)
- Create Images And Share Them (Passive & Proactive Link Building)
- Write Product Reviews And Get Linkbacks
- Ask For Backlinks
- Give Product And Software Out For Review
- Be First To The Market
- Search On Your Brand Or Website For Mentions

I have written a pretty inclusive list of backlink methods that you can employ. (http://hangtenseo.com/backlinks-20-inbound-marketing-methods/)

Localized Backlink Campaign

With a localized backlink campaign, you are only focused on local businesses to help boost your local SEO presence. You can employ many of the same technique as traditional backlink strategies, but you're Keeping It Local.

The goal is to increase local signals that will help get you to the top the local listings.

Citation Backlink Campaign

The goal of a citation backlink campaign is to boost the page authority for each citation's page, which in turn will boost your overall Citation Authority. This is often a step that is overlooked when pursuing Local SEO efforts and can be the difference between ranking number 1 and being lower on the list.

A side benefit of citation backlinking is you can actually boost your domain authority by having stronger authoritative citations.

In general, the Open Site Explorer by Moz (https://Moz.com) will give you a good starting baseline for your backlink campaign.

CHAPTER 13 – Social Media And Sharing

The goal of Social Media and Sharing is to drive traffic, gain popularity and increase both page rank (PA) and domain rank (DA). This in turn will help improve your overall local ranking.

Google and other search engines have included social signals as a ranking factor when determining both page and domain authority.

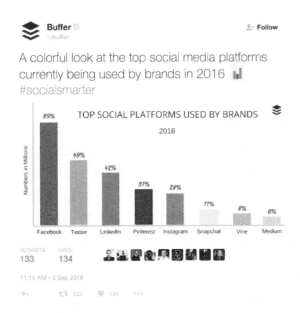

In the image above, you can see that the top 5 sharing platforms are:

- Facebook
- Twitter
- LinkedIn

- Pinterest
- Instagram

Having sharable content, videos and images are a big driving factor for successful social media campaigns.

The goal for most businesses should be to use Social Media to DRIVE traffic to their website on a regular basis rather than keeping the traffic on the specific social media platform.

There are many reasons for this, but a big one is because you don't have the ability to influence or control a social media company's decisions or policies.

If Twitter or Facebook or Instagram decide to make changes to their social platform that negatively effect your company, you're left with little to zero options to reverse such actions.

I am sure you have heard in the news when a Facebook account or Twitter account get suspended. The people who own those accounts literally are shut out and unless they have an alternate way to convey their brand or message, they are dead in the water.

So How Do You Go About Sharing?

First you must decide on a game plan and include things like:

- What Social platforms do I want to use?
- What type of information do I want to share?

- How often do I want to share it?

A lot of larger companies have social media specialists whose job it is to promote the company through social media. Smaller companies usually don't have that option, so they must focus on what works best for them given their resources or farm it out to a social media company.

Sharing can be sort of a pain if you perform it all manually. Luckily there are services like OnlyWire (https://onlywire.com/) that allow you to type one time and share across multiple social media accounts and networks.

The only downside to OnlyWire is you have to setup each social media account. That can take a few hours. For those who rather pay someone to do it, you can use services like Fiverr (http://Fiverr.com) to find someone to set the accounts up for you.

Make It Shareable

The ultimate social media success is if your content, image or video becomes a shareable asset, meaning people start to share it.

So how do you make something shareable? That's the $100,000 dollar question. Things that you think are shareable often aren't and things that you think nothing of - sometimes do get shared.

As a rule of thumb pictures and videos are very shareable, because of the visual aspect; so including images and videos that play on people's emotions or initiate some type of call to action are usually most shared.

There are loads of articles on how to make your content, images and videos more shareable. Here is a great article on shareable images to give you an idea on some great techniques.

(http://www.socialmediaexaminer.com/shareable-images/)

Top 6 Social Media Platforms

My advice is to be active on social media and use the social media platforms to drive traffic.

Without a doubt the following 6 social media platforms will help you boost traffic:

- Facebook
- Instagram
- LinkedIn
- Pinterest
- Twitter
- YouTube

Google now owns YouTube and without a doubt a YouTube account will help boost website traffic

Facebook and Twitter are excellent social media platforms to promote your brand and website.

Often overlooked, Pinterest has been shown to really drive traffic.

Hashtags And Keywords

A Hashtag is a word or phrase proceeded by a hash or pound sign (#) and is used to identify a message's topic.

Hashtags to help categorize messages, so that people can search specifically for messages that just pertain to that subject.

Hashtags are a great way to provide extra visibility for your posts and when used effectively can generate more buzz.

CHAPTER 14 – Evaluating A Business

When developing a Local SEO campaign for a business office, it's a good idea to evaluate the current status. In the SEO industry we call doing this an SEO Audit.

When I perform Local SEO audits I will have multiple tabs opened on my browser and use multiple tools to get a base line. The base line will set the tone for the entire campaign.

My current Local SEO tool lineup consists of:

- Moz Local – Check My Business (https://moz.com/local/search)
- Bright Local – Google Local Wizard (https://tools.brightlocal.com/seo-tools/admin/gpw)
- Google Maps (https://www.google.com/maps)
- Yelp (https://www.yelp.com)
- Google Analytics

Moz Local

Moz Local will give you a nice overview of what Moz considers the top citation providers broken down by:

- Primary Sources
- Direct Networks
- Indirect Networks

The listings are further broken down into:

- Complete - What citations have been created
- Incomplete – What citations need additional information
- Inconsistent – Which citations have conflicting address information
- Duplicates – What citations might need to be removed

All of these are important and should be reviewed.

You can tell right away whether you are working with a business that is brand new and doesn't have citations or one that is older with various degrees of citation information.

I can tell you from experience that almost every company I have audited needed citation help and most had their local SEO setup wrong.

BrightLocal

BrightLocal digs deeper into citation evaluation and not only gives you information on the business that you are reviewing, but also its competitors, based on keywords.

The BrightLocal Google Local Wizard report is broken down into:

- Top 10 Results
- Citation Matrix
- NAP Comparison (Your citation listing vs. Google's)
- Top Categories Used
- On Page Ranking Factors

Rank	Company Name	Citations	Citations Authority	Links	Website Authority	Reviews & (Rating)	📷	Categories
A	Bicycle Sport Shop ✓ Verified	166	50/100	21,524	45/100	186 (4.3/5)	22	Bicycle Shop
B	Austin Tri-Cyclist ✓ Verified	235	58/100	190	29/100	42 (4.1/5)	12	Bicycle store
C	Mellow Johnny's ✓ Verified	206	54/100	11,275	53/100	168 (4.3/5)	49	Bicycle Shop
D	Bicycle World ✓ Verified	272	55/100	24,413	39/100	66 (4.7/5)	2	Bicycle Shop
E	East Side Pedal Pushers ✓ Verified	207	60/100	30	23/100	56 (4.3/5)	11	Bicycle Shop
F	Fatz Fixies Cyclery ✓ Verified	77	58/100	168	29/100	36 (4.5/5)	11	Bicycle Repair Shop
G	Clown Dog Bikes ✓ Verified	74	56/100	180	22/100	69 (4.9/5)	9	Bicycle store
H	University Cyclery ✓ Verified	127	51/100	2	13/100	39 (3.9/5)	13	Bicycle store
I	REI ✓ Verified	230	47/100	261,711	87/100	139 (4.4/5)	18	Camping Store
J	Streamline Cycles ✓ Verified	28	74/100	2,147,483,647	100/100	11 (4.9/5)	40	Bicycle Rental Service

-- BrightLocal Top 10 Results --

The Top 10 results displays a high level view of your company vs. the competition in your area. It will show you exactly where the competition is leading in the citation building efforts.

-- BrightLocal Citation Matrix --

The citation matrix shows the number of citations, domain authority for each citation and what citations competitors are using.

This is such a fantastic amount of information. You can view the top competitor in your industry and see where their citations are listed and what domain authority each citation has.

-- BrightLocal Nap Comparison --

The NAP comparison compares your listing information to what is in Google My Business. It's more of a validation check.

-- BrightLocal Top 5 Categories --

Top 5 Categories displays top Google My Business categories. These categories, if not user created (Google changed the way categories can be added, which removed the ability to add user created categories) will help you improve your category lists for your business's Google My Business account.

-- BrightLocal Other Ranking Factors --

BrightLocal other ranking factors does a quick audit of your phone number and your landing page title tag to make sure the information is localized.

I absolutely love the information I get out of BrightLocal and it allows me to quickly gauge what work needs to be done to help improve the local authority score of the clients I work with and help boost their local presence.

Google Maps

I use Google maps to see what actually shows up for a business and where on earth it puts me. I can quickly see if the business is even listed, what, if any reviews they have, what pictures they have used and what information is listed.

Yelp

Another excellent source for citations is Yelp. Every business should have a Yelp listing. I will use Yelp to see if the company is listed in the city they are trying to rank for.

Reviews

While using both Google Maps and Yelp, I can easily see and read reviews on the business. I will often see limited reviews or a low review score when analyzing and auditing businesses, both of which are bad for Local SEO. Depending on the severity of the negative reviews or lack of reviews, I will often suggest creating a review campaign to raise number of reviews and score.

Google Analytics

For those that don't know, Google Analytics is Google's software for tracking website statistics including things like number of unique users, duration, bounce rate and much more.

It's important that every website have Google Analytics or some other type of website traffic tracking tool. The statistics allow you to gauge both current and past performance as well as help make sense of what is happening when people interact with a website.

Analytics will help present a clearer picture of campaigns that are being run and how effective they are at driving traffic.

I have run into several situations where Analytics hadn't been installed and in those cases you're somewhat starting from scratch.

CHAPTER 15 – Local SEO Checklist

To get you up and running fast by optimizing your businesses local presence and citation building efforts, I have included a Local SEO Checklist.

1. Optimize Your Website For Local Searches

    - Domain Name Selection (If possible include the city)
    - Create Local Business Page
    - Add Page Titles (Include the city on Home Page and Local Business Page)
    - NAP Listing (Use Schema Markup for address information)
    - Clean up broken links (404 errors)
    - Perform SEO Website Audit using SEOSiteCheckup.com or WooRank.com
    - Perform On-Page SEO Audit using Screaming Frog
    - Add Google Analytics.

2. Create Local Business Pages / Citations

    - Google My Business
    - Facebook
    - Yahoo
    - Bing

3. Perform Local SEO Audit

- Moz Local
- BrightLocal

4. Citation Building Campaign

- Manually Add Citations
- Moz Local (Citation Building Service)
- BrightLocal (Citation Burst Service)
- Yext (Citation Building Service)

5. Review Campaign

- Google My Business Reviews
- Yelp Reviews
- Facebook Reviews

6. Repeat Local SEO Audits (Weekly) and clean up any inconsistencies and duplications that are found.

- Moz Local
- BrightLocal

7. Local Business Campaign

- Whitespark (Find Local Citation listing providers)
- Local Businesses Outreach (Get involved in the local community to boost brand awareness and to build local backlinks)

VISIT MY WEBSITE:

HTTP://HangTenSEO.com